"*Girl Time* is a lovely and very heart-full mindfulness workbook for mothers and daughters. It will plant seeds of awareness and compassion, and will invite every girl to be curious and connected. Connectedness—to ourselves and to others—opens windows to really see, hear, feel, and touch each other's heart. May this book benefit many mothers and daughters."

—Eline Snel, author of *Sitting Still Like a Frog*

"*Girl Time* is an excellent resource for moms who want to stay connected to their daughters and empower them to stay connected to themselves. Dr. Snitbhan's creative, enjoyable, step-by-step activities offer experiences that help girls develop a strong core identity that is needed before transitioning into their teen years."

—Dr. Maria Clark Fleshood, author of *From Tweens to Teens*

"A treasure trove of activities that will inspire, educate, and connect mothers and daughters across the generational divide, and build happiness and emotional awareness for all."

—Dr. Christopher Willard, author of *Child's Mind*
and *Growing Up Mindful*

girl time

*A Shared Activity Book
for Girls and Their Moms
to Connect, Learn, and Love*

Girl Time

Nuanprang Snitbhan, PsyD

Illustrations by Lora Zorian

Shambhala *Boulder* 2016

Shambhala Publications, Inc.
4720 Walnut Street
Boulder, Colorado 80301
www.shambhala.com

© 2016 by Nuanprang Snitbhan, PsyD
Illustrations © 2016 by Lora Zorian

9 8 7 6 5 4 3 2 1

First Edition
Printed in the United States of America

♾ This edition is printed on acid-free paper that meets the American National Standards Institute Z39.48 Standard.
♻Shambhala Publications makes every effort to print on recycled paper. For more information please visit www.shambhala.com.
Distributed in the United States by Penguin Random House LLC and in Canada by Random House of Canada Ltd

Designed by Lora Zorian

Library of Congress Cataloging-in-Publication Data

Snitbhan, Nuanprang, author.
Girl time: a shared activity book for girls and their moms to connect, learn, and love /
Nuanprang Snitbhan, PsyD.—First edition.
pages   cm
Includes bibliographical references.
ISBN 978-1-61180-304-4
(pbk.: alk paper) 1. Mothers and daughters.
2. Parent and child. I. Title.
HQ755.85.S576 2016
306.874'3—dc23
2015025253

Contents

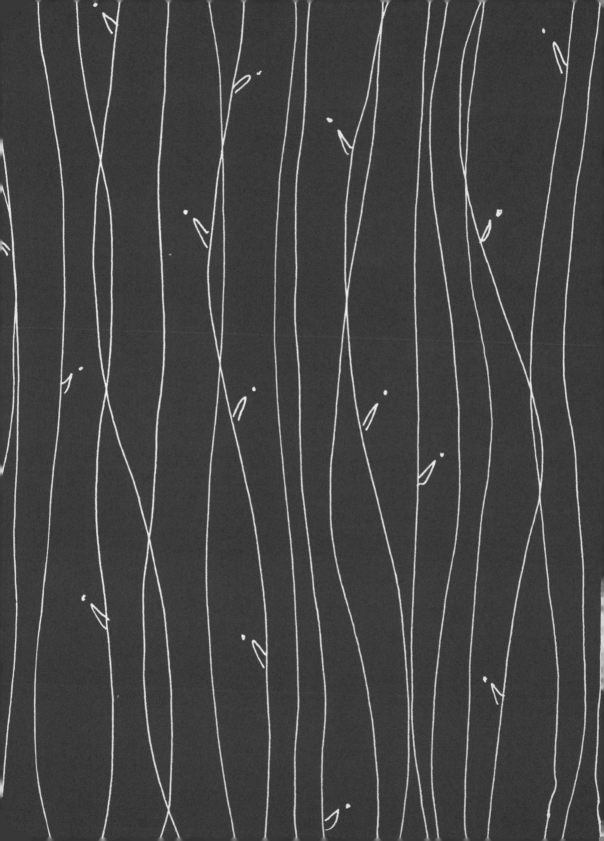

A Note to Daughters and Their Moms

Children have feelings and thoughts just like adults do. However, the big difference between children and adults is that children often have a harder time saying what they think or expressing how they feel. To some kids this can be frustrating and confusing. The truth is, your mom has more practice than you! Trust me, it's totally okay to be sensitive or to have strong feelings. There are so many advantages to that, and as you go through this book you'll find out what they are.

I've developed this workbook for you and your mom to do together, as a shared activity. Take turns completing the exercises in each chapter—and then share what you've written! My goal is for you to also learn some crucial life skills that can be hard to teach and also hard to talk about. You are not alone in thinking that there are a lot of topics that parents and kids avoid discussing—things that are strange, awkward, or uncomfortable to talk about, like anger, anxiety, and stress. Many parents don't know how to start a conversation on such topics, and so they hope that their kids will learn about these issues at school. At the same time, a lot of kids are afraid to ask questions or share their thoughts and feelings because they don't want their parents to worry about them or be on their backs. The good news is that by using this workbook, you and your mom will find it easier to connect and talk about difficult topics. I recommend that you do one activity a week so that there is enough time to practice your new skills. In the book, you will find questions that will help you share your feelings and thoughts with each other in ways that feel safe. All of the activities in this workbook will help you learn to take care of your body and mind, gain a sense of control, and think about things from new perspectives. You will also learn skills that you can use to become more mindful, happier, and healthier, and to have better relationships with the people around you.

I hope you will have fun and enjoy the time you spend together doing these activities and exercises. Don't forget to pay attention to the tips I added in the "Even More Mindful Ideas" sections and the different breathing exercises I introduce in "Let's Take a Breather" at the end of each activity. You will find even more creative ideas to help you stay connected and feel grounded in the "More Tools" section at the end of this workbook.

Get ready to have some fun!

girl time

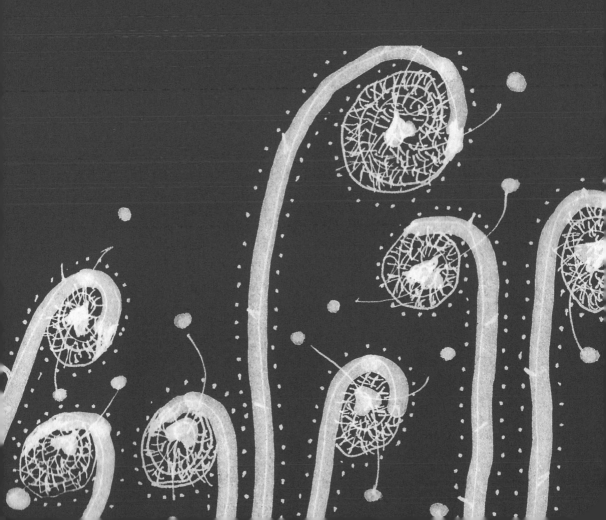

let's...Be Mindful

Mindfulness" is the practice of slowing down and paying attention to your breath or your surroundings, moment to moment, without thinking about the future or the past. It is a practice that people have been doing for thousands of years and that has proven to be beneficial to both children and adults. Maybe mindfulness sounds boring, confusing, or difficult to you. But if you just try it out, hopefully you'll find that it is none of those things. When you get good at it, it can make you happier, people will enjoy being with you even more, and you will be better able to handle the challenges life throws at you. Have you ever heard the expression "When life gives you lemons, make lemonade"? By practicing mindfulness, you will become the best lemonade maker in the world!

Mindfulness practice works like this: Imagine you are walking through a field of tall grass. When you walk through the field the first time, it's tricky—you have to step through the grass; it can be tough. But the next day when you walk through it, you can see your footprints, so it's easier to navigate. After weeks, and then months, the grass becomes a clear path with nothing blocking it, very easy and pleasant to walk on. This is just like practicing mindfulness—it gets easier each time you do it!

ABOUT THIS ACTIVITY

This first activity focuses on how to live in the present moment and increases your awareness of your surroundings and what is going on around you. Don't worry—it's fun! This particular exercise asks you to explore your kitchen and invites you to notice things around the house that you have never thought about much before. Throughout the book, there will be a variety of activities to help you step back and become more aware—not just of your surroundings but also of your thoughts, feelings, behaviors, and habits. At the end of each exercise you'll find a "Talk Time" section, where you and your mom will get a chance to share your work, thoughts, and feelings with each other. After that, a five-minute belly-breathing practice for mother and daughter to do together will help you end each activity with a calmer mind.

EVEN MORE MINDFUL IDEAS

You can practice being in the present moment by taking a break for a couple of minutes from what you are doing and focusing on what is going on around you. Pick one sense out of the five major senses— sight, hearing, smell, touch, and taste—and pay attention to it. Take five minutes to just listen to any noises around you. When your mind starts to wander, simply return to the task again.

Daughter: Becoming an Explorer

Take five minutes to look around the kitchen and write down in the space below as many round objects as you can find.

Take another five minutes to find different scents around your house and describe them here.

Once you are done, find a comfortable place to sit down with your mom to answer the questions in the Talk Time section on page 5.

Mom: Becoming an Explorer

Take five minutes to look around the kitchen and write down in the space below as many round objects as you can find.

Take another five minutes to find different scents around your house and describe them here.

Once you are done, find a comfortable place to sit down with your daughter to answer the questions in the Talk Time section on the next page.

Talk Time

How many round objects did you find in the kitchen? _____

Share your favorite scents with each other and draw some in the space below.

What did you learn from this exercise?

Let's Take a Breather

What does it mean to take a breather? It simply means to rest or take a break. Often we rush and jump from one thing to another, but it's really important to take a little time to pause and let things sink in after accomplishing something. It is also a really nice way to recharge your body and mind before moving on to the next task.

So daughter and mom can close each activity by spending a little quiet time together practicing five minutes of belly breathing. It's okay to use a timer, but it's not necessary. You should each find a comfortable space to relax—maybe on the sofa or in a chair that you like. You may open or close your eyes, but if you leave them open, it's best to pick a spot to focus your attention on. Or you can just rest your gaze toward the end of your nose. Take deep, slow, comfortable in-breaths through your nose and then let them out slowly through your mouth, like you're blowing big bubbles from your belly. As you breathe in, say to yourself, *I am breathing in,* and as you breathe out, say to yourself, *I am breathing out.*

let's ... Talk about Feelings

Research shows that all humans are born with eight basic emotions—joy, sadness, anger, fear, disgust, surprise, acceptance, and anticipation—but in the English language, we have more than four hundred words to describe emotions. That's a lot!

Do you know that feelings usually don't last that long? Pleasant feelings, neutral feelings, and unpleasant feelings—they come and go like waves in the ocean. People often try to avoid unpleasant feelings because they were told that negative feelings are bad. In reality, negative feelings are not bad, but how you act on them often leads to either a pleasant outcome or an unpleasant outcome. Knowing this means that every time a strong feeling pops up, you have a choice to make and you are responsible for it.

ABOUT THIS ACTIVITY

The exercise that follows asks you to simply watch and name your feelings. It's very important to accept your feelings rather than to try to change them, avoid them, or distract yourself from them. In this activity, you will be asked to come up with as many feelings as you can and then put them into one of three groups: a positive group, a neutral group, or a negative group. Since your mind and your body are connected, it's important to pay attention to your facial expressions and what they mean so that you can understand how others are feeling when they make similar expressions. Pay attention to the eyebrows, eyes, and mouth in particular.

The Feelings Chart at the end of this exercise is there to help you increase your feelings vocabulary. In the Talk Time section, you and your mom will get a chance to share what you both learned, and then you'll spend five minutes together breathing deeply from your belly. Have fun, and let your imagination run wild!

EVEN MORE MINDFUL IDEAS

Make copies of the Feelings Chart—as many as you need—and hang them around the house. Your refrigerator door, your bedroom, or your bathroom mirror might be good places to start. The goal is to help you notice and observe your feelings wherever you are.

Daughter: Name Your Feelings

Take three minutes to write down as many feelings as you can think of.

Look at your feelings list and decide which box each one belongs in:

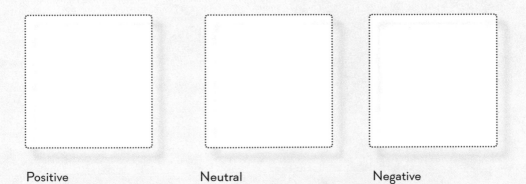

Positive   Neutral   Negative

Now think of four different animals and one feeling that goes with each animal.

For example, Crocodile & Afraid

_____ & _____

_____ & _____

_____ & _____

_____ & _____

Name three feelings you have the most, and then draw a face that expresses each feeling. Use a mirror if you want to see what you look like making that face.

1 _____   2 _____   3 _____

Share your work with your mom and answer the questions in the Talk Time section together.

Mom: Name Your Feelings

Take three minutes to write down as many feelings as you can think of.

Look at your feelings list and decide which box each one belongs in:

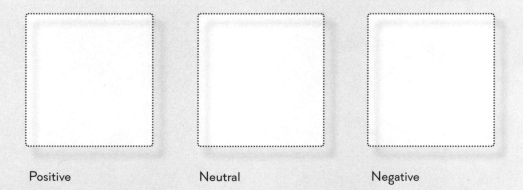

Positive   Neutral   Negative

Now think of four different animals and one feeling that goes with each animal.

For example, Crocodile & Afraid

_____ & _____

_____ & _____

_____ & _____

_____ & _____

Name three feelings you have the most, and then draw a face that expresses each feeling. Use a mirror if you want to see what you look like making that face.

1_____   2_____   3_____

Share your work with your daughter and answer the questions in the Talk Time section together.

The Feelings Chart

Talk Time

Draw or write down all the feelings that both of you came up with.

What feelings do you and your mom have in common?

Where would be a good place for you to hang up the Feelings Chart?

Let's Take a Breather

We will end this activity with a five-minute belly-breathing practice for mother and daughter to do together. Again, it's okay to use a timer but it's not necessary. Find a comfortable space to allow yourself to relax. You may open or close your eyes, but if you leave them open, it's better to pick a spot to focus your attention. Or you can just direct your gaze toward the end of your nose.

Take a slow, deep breath, filling up your belly—not your chest—with the air. Now let it out slowly from your belly, gently pulling your belly back in so you push the air out. Remember the idea that all feelings come and go. As you breathe into your belly, *accept* this idea, and as you breathe out, allow your body and mind to *relax*. If this doesn't work for you, you may also try to imagine a white warm light spreading all over your body to keep you warm, safe, and calm. Stay in place, and breathing like this, for five minutes. When you are done you can smile at each other or give each other a high five!

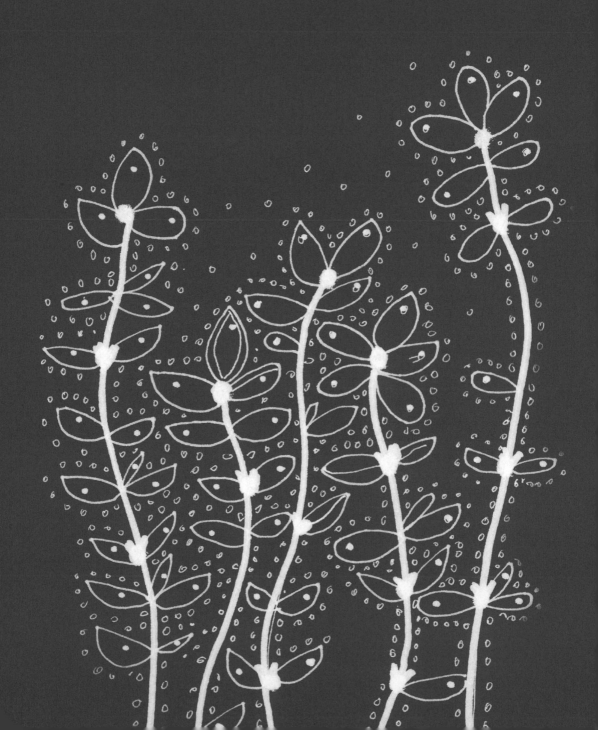

let's... Observe the Pleasant Feelings

Everyone generally agrees that happiness is the best feeling, and there are many ways to feel happy and grateful in life. Having a birthday can make you feel excited. Getting a good grade on a test can make you feel proud. Recovering from a cold or other sickness can make you feel relieved. Falling in love can make you feel giddy. Playing with a dog can make you feel joyful. Volunteering to help others in need can make you feel valued. Giving and receiving a hug can make you feel loved.

The source of happiness is different for different people, even for those who grew up in the same family. Why is it important for you to know where your happiness comes from and what makes you happy? Because when you're happy, you smile more, speak kindly, and act from that positive energy—and that makes you feel wonderful. It also makes other people feel happy and comfortable being around you.

ABOUT THIS ACTIVITY

This activity will bring you back to a happy time in your life. The first part of the activity gives you and your mom a chance to write or draw about a shared happy memory. You may not want to talk to each other until both of you are done. When you're finished, exchange your work. The second part asks you to describe your thoughts, feelings, or reactions after taking a look at the other person's work. Then, during the Talk Time section, you'll get a chance to come up with other good times you've had together. You will also learn to share your happiness with the world around you by setting an intention (goal) with your breath in the Let's Take a Breather section.

EVEN MORE MINDFUL IDEAS

Give yourself a chance to watch yourself being happy. You might want to add more happy memories of your own to your list. It is important to start noticing what warms your heart and makes you feel good inside.

Daughter: My Happy Memory

Use this space to write or draw the first happy memory that comes to your mind. Take time to enjoy this moment alone. You will share your work with your mom later.

All done! Swap your work with your mom. Now take a look at her story or drawing and write or draw how you think and feel about her work.

Feel free to come back to this exercise whenever you are down or stuck in a negative place, because when people are sad, they forget about good and positive things. This exercise can be used as a reminder that the world is not going to collapse on them today. Now, turn to the Talk Time section and answer some more questions there.

Mom: My Happy Memory

Use this space to write or draw the first happy memory that comes to your mind. Take time to enjoy this moment alone. You will share your work with your daughter later.

All done! Swap your work with you daughter. Now take a look at her story or drawing and write or draw how you feel and think about her work.

Feel free to come back to this exercise whenever you are down or stuck in a negative place, because when people are sad, they forget about good and positive things. This exercise can be used as a reminder that the world is not going to collapse on them today. Now, turn to the Talk Time section and answer some more questions there.

Talk Time

Good memories are so precious. Come up with a list of some other good times you've had together.

Let's Take a Breather

You can end this activity with a five-minute belly-breathing practice for mother and daughter to do together. Find a comfortable place to relax. You may close your eyes or keep them open, whatever feels best to you. Take a slow, deep breath, filling up your belly—not your chest—with air. Now let it out slowly from your belly, gently pulling your belly back in as you push the air out.

This breathing exercise is a little different from the ones in the previous two activities because this time you will share your happiness with the world around you by setting an intention (goal) with your breath. As you breathe in, imagine you are taking in all the *happiness* in the world, around you and within you. As you breathe out, send out *love*, *happiness*, and *peace* to all your family, your friends, and even to people who might not be your favorites. Do this with each breath until five minutes is up. When you are done you can smile at each other or give each other a high five!

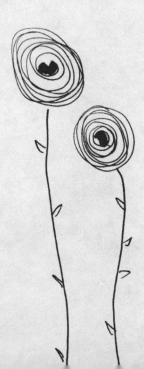

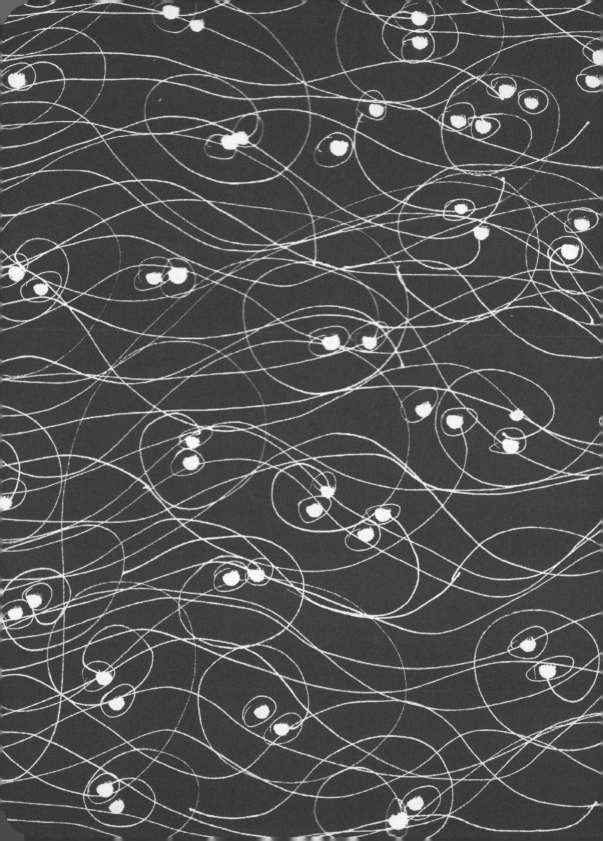

let's... Observe the Not-So-Good Feelings

It's natural to have all kind of feelings: positive, neutral, and negative. We talked about pleasant feelings in the last activity. Now let's talk about not-so-good feelings—negative feelings. Of course, negative feelings usually don't make you feel that great, and sometimes they can seem very big and overwhelming. It's much easier to avoid talking about and sitting with negative feelings because no one likes to be sad and miserable. Sure, avoiding talking about or paying attention to negative feelings can work for a little while; it gives you time to not think about them or face them. But the longer you avoid negative feelings, the bigger they become and the harder they are to handle. It's like a snowball: if you start rolling a small one down a snowy hill, by the time it gets to the bottom, it will be huge! This is what can happen with negative feelings if you don't take care of them. One day, you will explode. So the key to dealing with unpleasant feelings is to learn to accept them, understand them, and find strategies to release and work through them, either on your own or with the help of someone else.

ABOUT THIS ACTIVITY

The goal of this activity is for you and your mom to explore negative feelings and to become more comfortable with them. First, you'll each come up with a list of as many negative feelings as you can think of. Then you'll pick any feeling from the list and think of a situation or a time when you felt that way. During the Talk Time section, you and your mom will learn more about how your family handles negative feelings. After that, both of you will have a chance to practice breathing quietly together for a few minutes.

EVEN MORE MINDFUL IDEAS

Anytime a negative feeling pops up, try to remind yourself to just notice it. Watch your thoughts and actions, and see where it takes you.

Daughter: My Feeling Diary

What are your not-so-good feelings? Write down as many as you can think of.

Pick four feelings from your list above and write one on the top of each box below. Then in each box draw a picture or describe in a few words a time or a situation in which you experienced that feeling. For example, if you choose the feeling "frightened," you might draw a picture of thunder and lightning.

Mom: My Feeling Diary

What are your not-so-good feelings? Write down as many as you can think of.

Pick four feelings from your list above and write one on the top of each box below. Then in each box draw a picture or describe with a few words a time or a situation in which you experienced that feeling. For example, if you choose the feeling "frightened," you might draw a picture of thunder and lightning.

Talk Time

Thinking about negative feelings and sharing them with others can be difficult. Is it okay to talk about negative feelings in your family? If not, why not?

Each family finds different feelings hard to talk about. Which feelings does your family find hard to talk about?

When your feelings get big and uncomfortable, who do you find it helpful to talk to?

Let's Take a Breather

We'll end this activity with a five-minute belly-breathing practice for mother and daughter to do together. Find a comfortable space to allow yourself to relax. You can open or close your eyes like you did before.

Take a slow, deep breath, filling up your belly—not your chest—with air. Now let it out slowly from your belly, gently pulling your belly in so that you push the air out. Remind yourself that you are not your feelings. However, one important way to take care of big feelings is to let yourself sit with uncomfortable feelings rather than trying to forget, ignore, or avoid them. As you breathe in, *accept* this idea, and as you breathe out, allow your body and mind to *relax*. If this doesn't work for you, you may also try to imagine a white, warm light spreading all over your body to keep you warm, safe, and calm. Do this for the next five minutes.

During those difficult moments, try to remind yourself to listen to your feelings—you will have better control of the situation, feel good about yourself, and become a great problem solver! When you are finished with the breathing practice, smile at each other or give each other a high five.

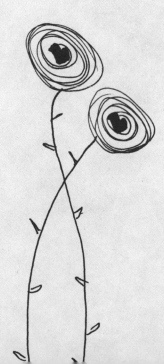

let's ... Observe Boredom

Our lives are so *busy*. We are always doing something or going somewhere. Some families have their weekends booked for weeks—even months—in advance, because often parents feel they need to keep their children constantly entertained. Forget about being bored; no one ever even has time to sit and relax or be alone! Does this sound familiar to you and your family at all?

Truthfully, boredom is necessary and can be a good thing for both children and adults. Learning to be alone is an important skill to acquire and cultivate—just like politely introducing yourself to new people, asking questions in class, or having good table manners. Research shows that children need unstructured time to practice self-directed play, which allows them to look inside themselves, learn to manage their free time, expand their imagination, explore their interests, creativity, and passions, and feel accomplished. Basically, children need to be given the opportunity to be bored.

ABOUT THIS ACTIVITY

You and your mom will each get an empty weekly schedule. Your job is to write down all the activities you have from Monday through Sunday, starting from 6 A.M. and going to 8 P.M. Color in one big block during the time you're at school or at work. After you're finished, you'll look at each other's schedules and talk about what you notice: pay particular attention to any downtime in your schedules. The last part of the activity will ask you to find time in your schedule to practice being alone and possibly be bored. Yes, you read that correctly! Make sure you pick a time and pencil it in.

Start with twenty minutes and once you master that, add more time. Over time, you will be surprised by what boredom can offer you. In the Talk Time section, you and your mom will get a better understanding of your daily routines, and, hopefully, you will learn to relax more when you are by yourself or feel bored. After that, you'll do a five-minute breathing practice to wrap up your amazing work!

EVEN MORE MINDFUL IDEAS

While practicing being alone, avoid all screens. You should turn off your TV, cell phone, iPod, iPad, and computer. Just watch your thoughts and see what you can come up with.

Daughter: Practice Being Alone

What does your weekly schedule look like? Fill in your regular routine and activities here. Turn to the Talk Time section when you finish.

	Mon.	Tues.	Wed.	Thurs.	Fri.	Sat.	Sun.
6 A.M.							
7 A.M.							
8 A.M.							
9 A.M.							
10 A.M.							
11 A.M.							
12 P.M.							
1 P.M.							
2 P.M.							
3 P.M.							
4 P.M.							
5 P.M.							
6 P.M.							
7 P.M.							
8 P.M.							

Mom: Practice Being Alone

What does your weekly schedule look like? Fill in your regular routine and activities here. Turn to the Talk Time section when you finish.

	Mon.	Tues.	Wed.	Thurs.	Fri.	Sat.	Sun.
6 A.M.							
7 A.M.							
8 A.M.							
9 A.M.							
10 A.M.							
11 A.M.							
12 P.M.							
1 P.M.							
2 P.M.							
3 P.M.							
4 P.M.							
5 P.M.							
6 P.M.							
7 P.M.							
8 P.M.							

Talk Time

Looking at your own schedule, what takes up most of your time?

How many hours of downtime do you have in your schedule? _____

Take a look at your schedule again and pencil in an electronic-free time that would be good to practice being alone. Start with twenty minutes, then increase the time slot to thirty minutes, then forty minutes, and so on. You can play, try out new recipes, or start a fun project. This time is for you to be alone, and it's okay to be bored or do nothing.

Let's Take a Breather

You and your mom can end this activity with a five-minute belly-breathing practice. Find a comfortable space to allow yourself to relax. You may open or close your eyes.

Take a slow, deep breath, filling up your belly—not your chest—with air. Now let it out slowly from your belly, gently pulling your belly back in so that you push the air out. Remind yourself that boredom is not a bad thing. As you breathe in, imagine and appreciate all the *freedom* that comes with boredom. As you breathe out, welcome *joy* and *creativity* into your life. If this doesn't work for you, try to imagine any color of light that you want spreading all over your body, to keep you open and free. Once you are done don't forget to smile at each other or give each other a high five.

Believe it or not, you have just learned an important life skill. From now on, whenever you feel bored, one of the things you can do is practice this breathing exercise. Boredom can be a good thing.

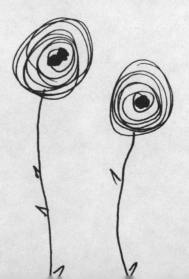

let's ... Observe Our Worry

It is normal for both kids and adults to worry or feel anxiety. Kids can get nervous and worry about things like the first day of school, making new friends, taking a test, seeing adults arguing, being in the dark, or going to the dentist. Actually, a normal level of anxiety can be a good thing: it can push you to try harder or keep you safe. For example, you may spend more time preparing for a math test because math is your least favorite subject, or you may look more carefully before you cross the street when you are alone than when you are with an adult. However, if you are worried a lot, you may start complaining that your stomach and head hurt, or that you have trouble falling asleep at night. Sometimes kids worry so much that they don't enjoy school and may refuse to go to school. This can happen to anyone, but there are ways to fix it—and for that reason, it is important to let an adult know if you are worried.

Two things to remember: one, being nervous or worrying about something a lot does not make you weak or a bad person. Chances are, many of the adults you know have probably had a time in their lives when they worried too much and had to work it out, either on their own or with the help of others. So they can share their experience with you and help you take care of the anxiety. Also, it's good for parents to know that it's usually not helpful to simply tell a worried person to stop thinking so much or worrying. It's best to accept other people's feelings of anxiety, listen carefully, and together find ways to gain control over those feelings.

ABOUT THIS ACTIVITY

This activity is designed to help both you and your mom to talk about anxiety in a way that makes you feel safe. Both of you will write a letter to Worrywart and express your feelings about your worry or anxiety by filling in the blank spaces. This exercise will help you learn more about your worry or anxiety and will give you a better idea of how to share it with someone you trust. During the Talk Time section, you and your mom will really get to think about your worry or anxiety in a different way that makes you feel stronger and bigger than you feel you are now. Then you will help each other come up with different ideas on how to beat your worry and anxiety and gain more control of your own mind. At the end of this activity, you will do another five-minute breathing practice with the goal of boosting your self-confidence by cultivating the inner strength and calmness that already exist within you.

EVEN MORE MINDFUL IDEAS

Identify a time or a situation that makes you worried or anxious. Remind yourself not to freak out, run away, or avoid it. (It tends to only get worse or last longer if you do.) Accept your worry and avoid judging yourself, a situation, or others! Notice your body sensations, your breathing pattern, your thoughts, and your behaviors when you feel worried or anxious.

Daughter: A Letter to Worrywart

There is no right or wrong answer here. Just fill in the blank spaces.

Dear Worrywart,

My name is _____ . I am ____ years old. I am really good at

_____ . I also enjoy _____ with my family. My

best friend, _____ , and I love _____ .

For the most part, I _____ school and _____ home.

My teacher thinks I am _____ . My mom thinks I am

_____ . But there is something I haven't really shared with

anyone. I don't really know why—maybe because I feel _____ . The

thing is, I sometimes worry about _____ . On a scale from 1 to

10 (1 = relaxed; 10 = extremely worried), I would probably give it a ___ .

When I think about _____ , it makes me _____ . In the

past, I _____ to make myself feel better or forget about it for a

while. Sometimes it worked, but sometimes it didn't.

Sincerely,

_____

Signature

Mom: A Letter to Worrywart

There is no right or wrong answer here. Just fill in the blank spaces.

Dear Worrywart,

My name is _____. I am ____ years old. When I was

young, I was really good at _____ . I remember I liked to

_____ with my family. My best friend, _____, and I

used to_____. We had so much fun together.

My childhood was _____. My teacher thought I was

_____. My mom said I was _____. But there

was something I didn't really share with anyone. I don't really know why;

maybe because I felt _____. The thing is, I used to worry about

_____. On a scale from 1 to 10 (1 = relaxed; 10 = extremely

worried), I probably gave it a ___. When I thought about _____, it used

to make me _____. However, what helped me the

most was _____.

Sincerely,

_____

Signature

Talk Time

If you were to give your worries a name, what would it be? If you were to give your worries a shape, what would it look like? Use the space below to get creative!

Talk about a time when you were worried and what you did to make it better. Tear out the next page and cut out the six cards, then write a few ideas of what you did to feel better then (such as writing it down in a notebook, watching a funny movie, etc.) you and your mom came up with on the back of each one. Keep them in a place where you can easily find them later (in a drawer, in your purse, on the refrigerator).

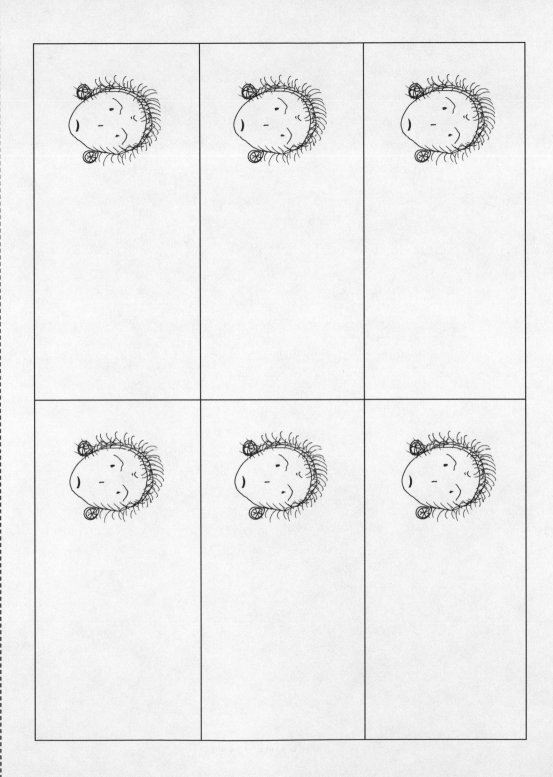

Let's Take a Breather

We will end this activity with a five-minute belly-breathing practice for mother and daughter to do together. Find a comfortable space to allow yourself to relax. You may open or close your eyes.

Take a slow, deep breath, filling up your belly—not your chest—with air. Now let it out slowly from your belly, gently pulling your belly back in so you push the air out. As you breathe in, imagine you are taking in all the *strength* and *calmness* around you. Let it loosen the tightness that the worry might put in your belly. As you breathe out, pretend that you are blowing out the *worry* (or use the creative name for your worries that you came up with in Talk Time). You can imagine the worry burning away like wood in a fireplace. When you are finished, smile at each other or give each other a high five!

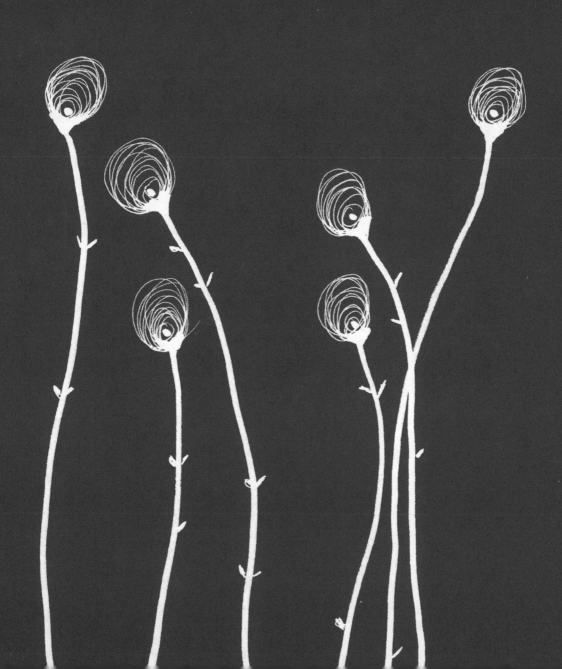

let's ... Talk about When Life Is Blue

Sadness is a natural human emotion. The truth is that no one can escape from being sad; all of us will experience sadness countless times during our lifetime. When people feel sad, they don't necessarily just sit quietly by themselves and cry. It is quite common for people who are sad to become angry or easily frustrated with others or with themselves.

Many different things can make us feel sad: not getting the grades we want, hearing some sad news or a sad song, moving to a new school, learning about a separation or divorce, finding out that someone has died, being bullied or watching someone get bullied, feeling lonely or out of control, and so on. The intensity of sadness is also different depending on the reason why you're sad. For example, you might feel a little sad when you find out that your favorite ice-cream shop closed down, but extremely sad when your dog dies. But when sadness lasts for too many days and it is hard to talk, play, eat, sleep, or have fun, it's important to let other people know and to ask for help. Trusted adults in your life can help you deal with sadness and to feel like your old self again.

ABOUT THIS ACTIVITY

This activity gives you and your mom a chance to think about and talk about what it's like to be sad. This is a very important conversation to have with someone you trust. Most people are afraid to talk about sadness because they worry it will just make them feel sadder. This activity will guide you in how to think and talk about sadness in a way that will help you understand it better and be able to spot it in others. The goal of this exercise is for you and your mom to walk away feeling much more confident about coping with sadness when it arises in the future. In the Talk Time section you will find a list of suggested activities that can come in handy for treating the blues. You'll find some good examples there to get you started. Again, you will end this activity with a five-minute breathing practice and learn to restore hope and surround yourself with family and friends who love and care about you when you're feeling blue.

EVEN MORE MINDFUL IDEAS

Sadness is not a comfortable feeling to experience, but it is very important that you learn to respect it and accept it. Watching yourself experience sadness without making any judgment is an important practice for mindful living.

Daughter: I Am Sad

Draw a sad face.

How can you tell when someone else is sad?

What kind of situation, person, or place makes you sad?

Normally, people experience a range of sadness that can be represented this way:

1   2   3   4   5   6   7   8   9   10

A little bit sad   Medium sad   Extremely sad

What situation would be a #1 for you? _____

What situation would be a #5 for you?_____

What situation would be a #10 for you?_____

How can other people tell when you are sad?

Share your work with your mom and turn to page 59, which includes a list of things you could do when you are sad. In the Talk Time section, you'll get a chance to make your own list.

Mom: I Am Sad

Draw a sad face.

How can you tell when someone else is sad?

What kind of situation, person, or place makes you sad?

Normally, people experience a range of sadness that can be represented this way:

1   2   3   4   5   6   7   8   9   10

A little bit sad   Medium sad   Extremely sad

What situation would be a #1 for you? _____

What situation would be a #5 for you? _____

What situation would be a #10 for you? _____

How can other people tell when you are sad?

Share your work with your daughter and turn to the next page, which includes a list of things you could do when you are sad. In the Talk Time section, you'll get a chance to make your own list.

Things to Do When Feeling Blue

Ride a bike

Color

Draw

Play a board game

Take a walk or jog

Sing

Go out for ice cream

Make a picture book

Kick a soccer ball

Eat chocolate

Read a funny story

Play with my favorite toys

Do a puzzle

Hug someone

Learn to make bracelets

Take a deep breath

Blow bubbles

Go on a nature hike

Think of positive things

Create a bouquet of flowers

Tell someone

Bake cookies

Shoot hoops

Climb a tree

Go skateboarding

Write it down

Volunteer

Ask for help

Play with a pet

Be kind to myself

Organize my room

Cry

Make cards

Play my instrument

Take a break

Wear soft clothes

Smile

Put on perfume

Watch a funny movie

Paint my nails a bright color

Listen to music

Practice yoga

Take a bath

Make homemade facial masks

Cook

Walk on grass with bare feet

Talk Time

Write down some ideas for activities you and your mom both might want to do when you feel "a little bit sad," "medium sad," and "extremely sad." Feel free to look at the list on the previous page for some suggestions.

A little bit sad

Medium sad

Extremely sad

Let's Take a Breather

You can end this activity with a five-minute belly-breathing practice for mother and daughter to do together. Find a comfortable space to allow yourself to relax. You may open or close your eyes.

Take a slow, deep breath, filling up your belly—not your chest—with air. Now let it out slowly from your belly, gently pulling your belly back in so that you push the air out. Remember, sometimes things in life can make us feel sad, and the reality is that we all have to experience that numerous times throughout our life. One great way to take care of yourself is to imagine taking in all the *hope* and *beautiful friendship* that you have in your life as you breathe in. Then, while breathing out, imagine all the *sadness* and *pain* you may experience in that moment leaving your body. When you are done you can smile at each other or give each other a high five!

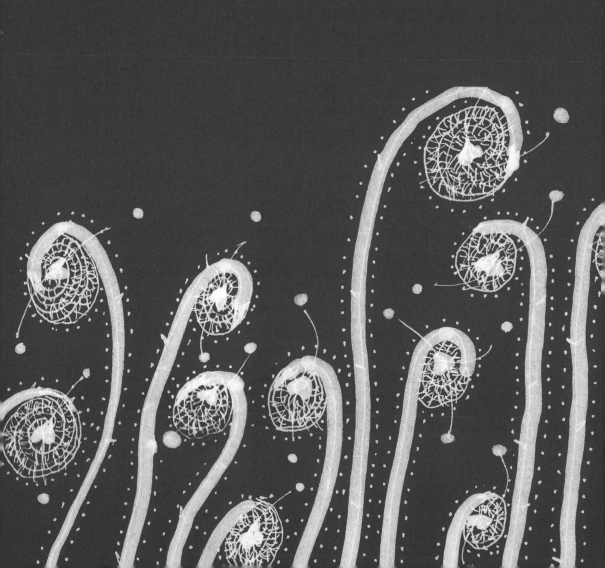

let's... Observe Anger

A lot of people get scared or nervous around an angry person because we are taught from a very young age that anger is a bad thing. But in reality, everyone gets angry. Anger is another normal human emotion that all of us experience when we don't get what we want or when someone is being nasty or unfair. If we stop and listen to our anger carefully, without judging it, it can actually teach us something about ourselves.

Usually when people get mad, they shut down and may do things outwardly to release tension, like yelling, throwing things, or arguing. These outward actions can make the angry person feel good for a short time, but as soon as they calm down, they often feel sorry and regretful about what they did. Has this ever happened to you? If the answer is yes, here is a way for you to consider dealing with your big anger.

The first step is to be aware of your feelings. Are you irritated? Are you frustrated? Are you angry? It sounds simple, but many people actually have a hard time figuring that out. It's very important and useful to learn to name and identify your specific feelings. Next, try to pay attention to your facial expressions, your tone of voice, your speech, your body, and your actions. All of these cues help you understand the intensity of your anger. Remember: having angry feelings is neither wrong nor bad; it's what you do with your anger that has the potential to lead to a bad result.

Many times when you act quickly without thinking, you end up feeling guilty or embarrassed, or getting into even more trouble. So the next time you are mad, you may want to practice catching yourself before you explode by breathing slowly and finding something else to do to distract yourself—such as riding your bike, getting a drink of water, smiling into a mirror, listening to music, or watching a movie. Once the fire inside you has cooled down, you will be in a much better state of mind to talk or to work things out in a mature and flexible way.

ABOUT THIS ACTIVITY

The goal of this activity is to show you how to slow down and be in control of your mind and body when you get angry. Focusing on your breath is an amazing tool. The more you practice using your breath, the better at it you will become—*and* you can concentrate on your breathing anywhere and anytime of the day. First, you will get to draw what the other person looks like when she is mad. Then, you will find belly-breathing mazes— one for you and another for your mom—which will guide each of you in your belly-breathing practice. Both you and your mom will take ten deep breaths so that you can really experience deep breathing. During the Talk Time section, both of you will spend time designing your own breathing log. You will also find another copy of the belly-breathing maze at the end of this activity. Save it and copy it as a tool to use in the future whenever you want to have more control over the anger monster inside you. Spend the last five minutes practicing breathing out your anger and breathing in the love and kindness around you.

EVEN MORE MINDFUL IDEAS

Make lots of copies of the belly-breathing maze and keep them in a spot that you will remember. A daily belly-breathing practice will make you feel better, happier, and calmer. When you catch yourself getting angry, remind yourself to breathe in all the *love* and *kindness* around you and slowly breathe out your *anger* and *pain*.

Daughter & Mom: What Does Your Mad Face Look Like?

When people get mad, they may show it in different ways. Use the circles below to draw what the other person looks like when she is mad.

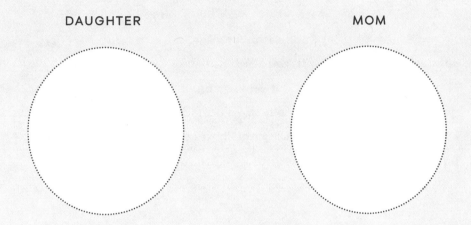

DAUGHTER

MOM

Daughter: Belly-Breathing Maze

The belly-breathing maze is a tool for focusing on the breath, a good way to slow yourself down and calm your mind. On the following page there is a random assortment of numbers 1 through 10, and the words "in" and "out." Your task is to take ten deep breaths from your belly as you draw connecting lines in the maze: as you breathe in, connect the number you're on to the word "in," and as you breathe out, extend the line farther to connect the word "in" with the word "out." For example, the first breath will be "1-in-out," then "2-in-out," and so on. It's okay to cross lines, but try to use a different "in" and "out" if you can. Note that it's more effective to breathe out longer than you breathe in; try to empty your belly as much as possible when breathing out.

In   In   7   Out   4

Out   In   1   !   Out

!   In   Out   6

9   Out   In   Out   10

2   In   !   !   In   Out

3   In   !   Out   8

Out   In   In   Out   5

Mom: Belly-Breathing Maze

The belly-breathing maze is a tool for focusing on the breath, a good way to slow yourself down and calm your mind. On the following page there is a random assortment of numbers 1 through 10, and the words "in" and "out." Your task is to take ten deep breaths from your belly as you draw connecting lines in the maze: as you breathe in, connect the number you're on to the word "in," and as you breathe out, extend the line farther to connect the word "in" with the word "out." For example, the first breath will be "1-in-out," then "2-in-out," and so forth. It's okay to cross lines, but try to use a different "in" and "out" if you can. Note that it's more effective to breathe out longer than you breathe in; try to empty your belly as much as possible when breathing out.

In   In   7   Out   4

Out   In   1   !   Out

!   In   Out   6

9   Out   In   Out   10

2   In   !   !   In   Out

3   In   !   Out   8

Out   In   In   Out   5

Talk Time

Talk to each other about how to use the space below to design your own weekly or monthly belly-breathing log. You and your mom will keep a record of how often you practice belly breathing, and you will also discuss how you would like to reward yourselves for mastering this new skill. On the next page you will find a fresh copy of the belly-breathing maze. Make more copies of it for future use.

Scales at the beginning and end of the page are there to help you pay closer attention to your feelings before and after the breathing exercise.

Belly-Breathing Maze

Date _____   Time _____

I feel _____

1	2	3	4	5	6	7	8	9	10
Calm				Frustrated					Angry

In   In   7   Out   4

    Out   In   1   !   Out

    !   In   Out   6

  9   Out   In   Out   10

2   In   !   !   In Out

  3   In   !   Out   8

    Out   In   In   Out   5

1	2	3	4	5	6	7	8	9	10
Calm				Frustrated					Angry

Let's Take a Breather

We will end this activity with a five-minute belly-breathing practice for mother and daughter to do together. Find a comfortable space to allow yourself to relax. You may open or close your eyes.

Take a slow, deep breath, filling up your belly—not your chest—with air. Now let it out slowly from your belly, gently pulling your belly back in so that you push the air out. As you breathe in, imagine you are taking in all the *love* and *kindness* around you. As you breathe out, pretend you are blowing out the *anger* and *hurt* that you may experience in that moment. You may try to imagine the *anger* and *hurt* falling away like drops of water in a river going over a waterfall. When you are done you can smile at each other or give each other a high five!

let's ... Talk about Stress

Do you know what being "stressed out" feels like? Many people are stressed without knowing it. Stress happens when you are in a situation that makes you feel overwhelmed, pressured, threatened, or out of control. These situations will often make you feel uncomfortable, worried, scared, or upset. Similar to anxiety or anger, a little amount of stress is actually necessary to make you work harder, get things done, and prepare you for challenging tasks. But too much stress is definitely not a good thing, and it can really make you feel not at all like yourself. The first rule of thumb for managing stress is to make sure you get plenty of sleep at night, eat healthy food, and exercise regularly.

Even though people experience stress differently, many people hold stress in their body, so it gets expressed through physical sensations like headaches, stomachaches, dizziness, sweaty hands, a pounding heart, and so forth. Some people exhibit stress through their actions or habits, like biting their nails, getting angry a lot, drinking alcohol, smoking cigarettes, eating a lot of junk food, or fighting with others. Therefore, it is important to be aware of how your body reacts to stress so that you can learn to respond to it quickly by being kind and gentle to yourself.

ABOUT THIS ACTIVITY

The goal of this activity is to teach you about stress and how it shows up in your body, mind, and behavior. On page 77 you will see a bunch of physical and emotional symptoms, feelings, and behaviors that stressed-out people sometimes experience. Your job is to try to think of a time when you felt overwhelmed, out of control, or stressed—for instance, when you had to perform in front of a lot of people, or when you argued with someone or heard people arguing, or when you did something wrong or felt left out—and then try to imagine what your body told you. Some people can remember these feelings clearly and some can't, and that's okay. During the Talk Time section, you and your mom will learn more about what makes each other stressed, and then you'll use the breathing practice to manage and reduce stress.

EVEN MORE MINDFUL IDEAS

If you know how your body responds to stress, notice the sensations and start taking care of yourself. If you don't, this is a good opportunity for you to pay attention to your body sensations, your behavior, and your mind so that you learn to live in the present moment and become more mindful.

Daughter: Where Does Your Stress Live?

People experience stress differently. Let's find out where in your mind, body, or behavior your stress expresses itself. In the list below, circle the things that happen frequently to you and draw a star next to those that happen sometimes.

CRYING   BORED

ARGUING   MOODY

WORRYING   BAD DREAMS

UNABLE TO EAT   STOMACHACHE

TEETH GRINDING   TIGHT MUSCLES

EATING TOO MUCH   SLEEP PROBLEMS

BITING FINGERNAILS   RAPID HEARTBEAT

DRY MOUTH OR THROAT   UNABLE TO CONCENTRATE

Share with your mom what you learn from this exercise and then go on to the Talk Time section.

Mom: Where Does Your Stress Live?

People experience stress differently. Let's find out where in your mind, body, or behavior your stress expresses itself. In the list below, circle the things that happen frequently to you and draw a star next to those that happen sometimes.

CRYING	BORED
ARGUING	MOODY
WORRYING	BAD DREAMS
UNABLE TO EAT	STOMACHACHE
TEETH GRINDING	TIGHT MUSCLES
EATING TOO MUCH	SLEEP PROBLEMS
BITING FINGERNAILS	RAPID HEARTBEAT
DRY MOUTH OR THROAT	UNABLE TO CONCENTRATE

Share with your daughter what you learn from this exercise and then go on to the Talk Time section.

Talk Time

Help each other learn more about the things that make you feel stressed. These things may be different for each of you, but some may also be similar. The first step is to recognize where your stress comes from. In the columns below, make a check mark beside the events, situations, or tasks that are potential sources of stress to you.

EVENT	DAUGHTER	MOM
Morning and bedtime routines		
Changing schools or jobs		
Fighting or disagreeing with others		
Having a busy schedule		
Illness or injury		
Death of a loved one		
Separation from loved ones		
Test or deadline		
Not fitting in		
My body		
Bad grades or evaluation		
Moving		
Holidays		
Homework		
Divorce		
New family member		
Siblings		
Bullying		
Performance or presentation		

Let's Take a Breather

We will end this activity with a five-minute belly-breathing practice for mother and daughter to do together. Find a comfortable space to allow yourself to relax. You may open or close your eyes.

Take a slow, deep breath, filling up your belly—not your chest—with air. Now let it out slowly from your belly, gently pulling your belly back in so you push the air out. As you breathe in, say "relax," and as you breathe out, say "let go." With each out-breath, imagine blowing out the stress from each part of your body. Start with your head, neck, shoulders, and arms. Next, imagine the stress leaving your chest. In the next breath, it leaves your belly without any tightness, then your bottom and thighs. Finally it leaves your legs and feet. Then start over until the five minutes are up. When you are done you can smile at each other or give each other a high five!

let's... Train Our Brain

Do you know that our brain has the capacity to change, grow, and adjust throughout our lifetime? Scientists have observed that new neurons are formed every day when we learn new things or perform challenging tasks, while old ones die naturally or from stress, injury, or disease. This process is called "brain plasticity." Of course, this does not mean that our brain is made out of plastic; it just means that human brains are flexible, not fixed and static.

Since our brain is constantly being reshaped and rewired by our day-to-day experience, we actually have the power to make a real impact on our brain. Many studies have proven that a simple way to train and rewire our brain is by concentrating on something or thinking about something repeatedly for a period of time. So if we train ourselves to think good thoughts and concentrate on positive things, our brain will start detecting lots of positives. On the flip side, if we focus our attention on negative things around us, our brain will learn to grab on to the negatives. Over time, these neuronal connections will become permanent and automatic, meaning that the positive-thinking people will be much happier than the negative-thinking people. So would you like to have a super healthy, mindful brain, or a depressed, grumpy, mindless brain? It's a choice you can make! What do you think?

ABOUT THIS ACTIVITY

In this activity, you and your mom will learn a simple technique for training your brain, to change the way you think, and to have more control over your thoughts and feelings. This is no joke—it is actually very true and very scientific! On the next page you will find a couple of statements for you to choose. Pick one that applies to you the most accurately and then seriously think about it for a couple of minutes. This exercise is meant to be done quietly and by yourself. The key is to try to concentrate on the meaning of the sentence and think about it over and over again instead of just merely copying it. The more you think about it, the quicker the neurons in your brain will form, shift, and reconnect. Once you are finished, you and your mom will help each other brainstorm ideas for how to train your brain to think positively about yourselves, correct negative thinking habits, and become the person you choose to be. To let the new information sink in, end this activity with a five-minute breathing practice. Hooray!

EVEN MORE MINDFUL IDEAS

Pick a statement that would make you a happier and kinder person; then really concentrate on its meaning. Be mindful of what you want to accomplish, and set up a time each day to dedicate to regular practice.

Daughter: Brain in Training

Isn't it cool to know that we have the power to control our brain? By concentrating on something or thinking about something over and over again, your brain will start forming new connections. The more you do it, the more success you will have. Let's start now! In the blank space below, copy one of the following sentences by hand as many times as you can in five minutes. If you run out of space, get another piece of paper.

I am special.

I am awesome.

If I try, I can do it.

It's okay to not be perfect.

It's okay to take risks!

Mom: Brain in Training

Isn't it cool to know that we have the power to control our brain? By concentrating on something or thinking about something over and over again, your brain will start forming new connections. The more you do it, the more success you will have. Let's start now! In the blank space below, copy one of the following sentences by hand as many times as you can in five minutes. If you run out of space, get another piece of paper.

I am special.

I am awesome.

If I try, I can do it.

It's okay to not be perfect.

It's okay to take risks!

Talk Time

Think of at least one word or sentence (and as many as ten) that you would like to write in the future to train your brain. Write it in one of the spaces below.

DAUGHTER	MOM

Let's Take a Breather

We will end this activity with a five-minute belly-breathing practice for mother and daughter to do together. Find a comfortable space to allow yourself to relax. You may open or close your eyes.

Take a slow, deep breath, filling up your belly—not your chest—with air. Now let it out slowly from your belly, gently pulling your belly back in so that you push the air out. Remember, you have the power to train and rewire your brain to become a healthy, more positive, and happier person. As you breathe in, remind yourself to think *healthy thoughts* and as you breathe out pretend to blow out any *unhealthy thoughts* that make you sad, nervous, or less confident. You can also imagine the unhealthy thoughts getting carried farther and farther away like a lost balloon in the sky. Practicing this exercise regularly can really make a big change in your life. When you are done you can smile at each other or give each other a high five!

let's…Relax

The human body consists of approximately thirty trillion cells. Each cell does a few million things per second to keep us alive. Each cell also has to know what every other cell is doing—otherwise our body would fall apart. Even though the human body is itself a miracle, we still need to do a lot to take care of it so that we stay healthy and happy.

Our mind and body are connected: our body often responds to how we think and feel even without our awareness. For example, imagine seeing a snake in the woods while walking your dog. What happens to your body? You sweat automatically. Your heart starts to pound harder. Blood flows toward the main organs and leg muscles so that you're prepared to move quickly away from whatever you perceive as a threatening situation. These bodily changes happen naturally and rapidly to keep us safe and alert. So learning to notice what our body is telling us is the first step toward understanding our feelings.

ABOUT THIS ACTIVITY

This activity is a joint activity. You and your mom will complete a scrambled list together. The body-scan activity will introduce you to different muscle groups in your body. To get to know your body even better, you will learn how to do a muscle relaxation exercise by tensing and relaxing one muscle group at a time. During this task, pay attention to your body and your breath. It's fine if some muscles are more relaxed or tense than others. If you feel some pain, just notice it, breathe a little longer, and move on. This might sound strange, but our feelings can get stored and stuck in our bodies and create pain, tightness, or muscle tensions. In the Talk Time section, you and your mom will get to answer a few more questions that will help you become more aware of where your feelings live in different parts of your body. The five-minute breathing practice afterward will help you end this activity with a new awareness of your body.

EVEN MORE MINDFUL IDEAS

Schedule a regular time to practice a body-scanning exercise. By paying attention to your bodily sensations, thoughts, and feelings, you begin to live mindfully, in the present moment.

Daughter and Mom: Body-Scan Scrambled List

1. After soccer practice, I told my mom that I wanted to rest my eyes. I went to my room and lay down on my _____.

2. My _____ are sore from my track meet last night.

3. When I get nervous, my heart beats fast, making my_____ go up and down.

4. People can guess what I am feeling by looking at my _____ and my body language.

5. I enjoy walking bare_____ on the sand.

6. When my grandma comes to visit, she wraps her_____ around me in one great big hug.

7. My _____ become tired after I write for a long time.

8. My_____ hurt after walking up so many stairs yesterday.

9. When people are stressed, it is normal for their_____ to become tight.

10. During the road trip, I had to sit on my_____ for five straight hours.

11. Sitting in front of the computer for a long time can make your neck and _____ stiff.

12. My _____ feels funny when I am scared or worried about some-thing.

ANSWERS:

stomach	neck	arms	chest
shoulders	thighs	foot	calves
bottom	hands	face	back

Muscle Relaxation Activity

The goal of the scrambled list was to introduce you and your mom to the major muscle groups in your body. Now that you have identified the muscle groups, you and your mom will learn how to relax your entire body by following these five steps.

STEP 1

Tense each muscle group for four seconds. Start with your face and work down to your feet—that is, face, neck, left shoulder, right shoulder, left arm, right arm, left hand, right hand, chest, stomach, back, bottom, left thigh, right thigh, left calf, right calf, left foot, right foot.

STEP 2

When you're finished, tense your whole body and hold it for four seconds. Don't stop breathing. Continue to breathe normally when you tense up: in through the nose, out through the mouth.

STEP 3

Let the tension or energy out really loud: HA! Then breathe normally again: in through the nose, out through the mouth.

STEP 4

Next, pick a place where you and your mom can lie down together for a few minutes. Once you get there, rest on your back next to each other. Close your eyes.

STEP 5

Now practice scanning your body from face to feet. Pay attention to each part of your body, simply noticing what it feels like. If you get to a spot where it feels tight or painful, it's okay to just stay there for a few breaths longer before you move on.

When you finish, turn to the next page to answer a few more questions.

Talk Time

Does your body feel relaxed or tight anywhere in particular?

Try to imagine yourself being in a happy place. Where do you feel it in your body?

Try to imagine yourself being in an angry, or sad, or scary place. Where do you feel it in your body?

Let's Take a Breather

We will end this activity with a five-minute belly-breathing practice for mother and daughter to do together. Find a comfortable space to allow yourself to relax. You may open or close your eyes.

Take a slow, deep breath, filling up your belly—not your chest—with air. Now let it out slowly from your belly, gently pulling your belly back in so you push the air out. As you breathe in, tell yourself to *relax*, and as you breathe out, tell yourself to *relax more*. You may also try to imagine yourself getting soaked up in a warm tub with nice-smelling lavender or vanilla oil, feeling super relaxed and calm. When you are done you can smile at each other or give each other a high five!

let's … Plant the Seeds of Positive Thinking

You've learned from many activities that your mind and body are connected. Your body and mind are constantly communicating and exchanging information, even when you are asleep. Sometimes you're aware of the connections, but other times you miss them. That's okay. It's actually normal. Similarly, your thoughts and feelings are also tied to each other. This might sound strange at first and can be a difficult concept to grasp, but once you start observing it, you'll get it.

Most people are aware of their feelings before they are aware of their thoughts; feelings are louder and more obvious, while thoughts often happen so quickly that you don't even know you had them. For example, if someone laughs at you, you may feel sad, happy, or embarrassed, depending on how you interpret the situation. If you think that they think you're stupid, you'll probably feel sad. If you think they laughed at your joke, you'll probably be happy. But if you think they laughed at your new pair of pants, you'll probably feel embarrassed. Can you see how thoughts can really influence your feelings? Again, it's harder to notice your thoughts than to recognize your feelings, unless you've been practicing. If you want to be happy and live mindfully, learn to pay attention to your thoughts. The secret is that you can change the way you feel by changing the way you think. Positive thinking makes you happy; negative thinking makes you miserable. It is as simple as that!

ABOUT THIS ACTIVITY

The goal of this activity is to train your mind to pay attention to the positive things around you, things that are simple and basic, but good. You and your mom will use this time to think of little things that make you smile, relax, and feel happy. Don't think too hard. Remember, there is no right or wrong answer here. It is all about what you like and enjoy. During the Talk Time section, share with each other what you came up with and what you learned about each other today. Then go ahead and enjoy five minutes planting the seeds of positive thinking by doing the breathing practice together.

EVEN MORE MINDFUL IDEAS

Practice this simple exercise every day and you'll start noticing more positive things in your life. You can start keeping a diary cataloging positive things and add more great ideas in there.

Daughter: Small and Simple

Most people forget about the little things in life that warm their heart, make them giggle, and bring them positive energy. It's almost a habit that we need to learn and practice over time until it becomes natural and automatic. Take this time to think of a few small and simple things that you appreciate, and write one on each petal of the flower below—for example, raindrops, a cup of hot chocolate, walking barefoot on the grass, watching clouds, and so on.

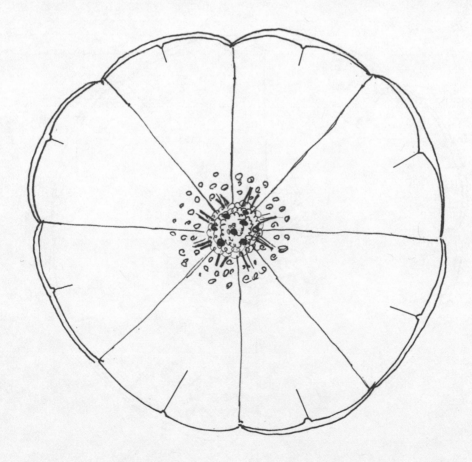

Mom: Small and Simple

Most people forget about the little things in life that warm their heart, make them giggle, and bring them positive energy. It's almost a habit that we need to learn and practice over time until it becomes natural and automatic. Take this time to think of a few small and simple things that you appreciate, and write one on each petal of the flower below—for example, raindrops, a cup of hot chocolate, walking barefoot on grass, watching clouds, and so on.

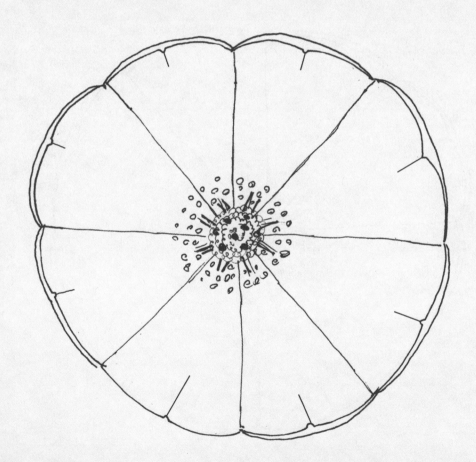

Talk Time

Was this exercise easy or hard for you? Share your experiences with each other.

Are there any small and simple things that one of you came up with that the other especially likes?

Do you think that it would it be helpful for your family to find a time every evening or every week to tell each other what small or big things you each are grateful for, or appreciative of?

Let's Take a Breather

We will end this activity with a five-minute belly-breathing practice for mother and daughter to do together. Find a comfortable space to allow yourself to relax. You may open or close your eyes.

Take a slow, deep breath, filling up your belly—not your chest—with the air. Now let it out slowly from your belly, gently pulling your belly back in so you push the air out. As you breathe in, imagine giving *happiness* and *love* to all your family, your friends, and even people who might not be your favorites. Make sure you allow yourself to experience the joy of being a giver. When you are done you can smile at each other or give each other a high five!

let's ... Exercise

Everyone knows that exercise is good for you. Not only does it keep you healthy and fit, it can also help improve your mood and reduce anxiety and stress. How much exercise is good for kids? School-age children should engage in some kind of physical activity every day for at least one hour. Getting enough exercise helps kids to learn faster, sleep better at night, raise their self-confidence and self-esteem, develop stronger and healthier bones and muscles, stay in shape, and ease stress.

In today's world, it's hard to say no to screen media. Kids spend hours and hours in front of the TV; they play video games, watch YouTube videos, look up things on their iPads, and text friends and listen to music on their smartphones. All of these activities are not so bad if they are done with supervision and in moderation. School-age kids should not stay in one position or be inactive for more than two hours at a time, except when they are asleep. It's the parents' responsibility to be good role models for an active and healthy lifestyle.

ABOUT THIS ACTIVITY

The purpose of this activity is for you and your mom to have fun exercising together. You'll find a list of exercises on the next page that you can both do, with options for activities inside and outside the house. The list will help you start thinking about fun exercises that you would like to do together. It's totally fine to start low-key, but then you should try stepping out of your comfort zone and challenging yourself a little bit. During the

Talk Time section, each of you will pick one activity from the list and mark a date to do it on your calendar so that it doesn't become just a wish or a dream. Then practice belly breathing for five minutes together. Work hard, play hard, and sweat more!

EVEN MORE MINDFUL IDEAS

Whatever exercise you choose to do, you should take a few minutes to concentrate on any movements, thoughts, feelings, or sensations that come up while you do it. Watch how your thoughts and feelings come and go like waves in the ocean.

Daughter: Our To-Do List

Things I like to do with you (circle each one):

- Play soccer
- Jump rope
- Go for a walk
- Play catch
- Swim
- Skate
- Play tennis
- Do yoga or stretching exercises
- Dance in the kitchen
- Play hide-and-seek
- Run up and down the stairs
- Go boating (canoeing, kayaking, sailing, rowing, paddleboating)
- Play Frisbee
- Ride bikes
- Play badminton
- Play volleyball
- Ride scooters
- Have a Hula-Hoop contest
- Work out to Gold's Gym Wii
- _____
- _____

When you finish, share your list with your mom. Notice any similarities and differences, then move on to the Talk Time section.

Mom: Our To-Do List

Things I like to do with you (circle each one):

- Play soccer
- Jump rope
- Go for a walk
- Play catch
- Swim
- Skate
- Play tennis
- Do yoga or stretching exercises
- Dance in the kitchen
- Play hide-and-seek
- Run up and down the stairs
- Go boating (canoeing, kayaking, sailing, rowing, paddleboating)
- Play Frisbee
- Ride bikes
- Play badminton
- Play volleyball
- Ride scooters
- Have a Hula-Hoop contest
- Work out to Gold's Gym Wii
- _____
- _____

When you finish, share your list with your daughter. Notice any similarities and differences, then move on to the Talk Time section.

Talk Time

Pick one or two activities from your lists to enjoy with each other this week. Be sure to schedule a date and time for each one.

Activity 1: Daughter

_____

Activity 2: Mom

_____

Date/Time

_____

Date/Time

_____

Let's Take a Breather

We will end this activity with a five-minute belly-breathing practice for mother and daughter to do together. Find a comfortable space to allow yourself to relax. You may open or close your eyes.

Take a slow, deep breath, filling up your belly—not your chest—with air. Now let it out slowly from your belly, gently pulling your belly back in so that you push the air out. As you breathe in, say to yourself, *I am breathing in,* and as you breathe out, say to yourself, *I am breathing out.* When you are done you can smile at each other or give each other a high five!

let's ... Eat

Most people eat three meals a day, but breakfast is the most important meal of the day for both kids and adults. It helps us recharge our brain and body and start the day feeling fresh and energetic. Skipping breakfast is like not filling your car with gas: eventually the tank will be empty and the car will stop running.

Most moms think a lot about what to feed their kids. It's a big responsibility to make sure that young people have a balanced diet that draws from a variety of food groups so that kids are ready to learn and play, and so they have strong immune systems. Have you heard the saying "You are what you eat"? This just means that the food you eat has a big impact on your body, mind, and overall well-being. Our eating habits usually stay with us into adulthood, so it's good to be aware of them early on and to change them if necessary. Do you know that some foods put you in a good mood and give you great energy, but other kinds of food can make you sleepy and tired? If you don't know much about this, that's completely fine because you will learn about it right now!

When you are busy playing and working, it's very easy to forget to drink water and stay hydrated. Water is important to help your body digest and absorb nutrition. So remind yourself to drink extra water after playing or engaging in any physical activity.

One last tip is to pay attention to your craving when you watch commercials on TV, because their job is not to make you stronger or healthier but to make you buy their products. To become a smarter eater, all you need is a healthy curiosity about food.

ABOUT THIS ACTIVITY

You and your mom will learn fun facts about the food that you eat every day or that you see in the grocery store. By the end of this activity, you will know more about what types of food help improve your mood, memory, and energy, and even your immune system. Before you start, make sure you have red, yellow, and green colored pencils, crayons, or markers: there will be some fun coloring coming up. During the Talk Time section, you will be able to talk more about your family's food preferences and maybe develop healthier ones using what you learn in this chapter. The belly-breathing practice at the end of this activity will help you transition smoothly into the rest of your day.

EVEN MORE MINDFUL IDEAS

Practice eating quietly. Turn off all the distractions: TV, phone, radio, and so forth. Pay attention fully to all the sensations you experience while eating.

Daughter: Food Boosters

Different foods have various vitamins, minerals, and properties that can have a specific effect on your body when you eat them. For example, many fruits and vegetables contain antioxidants, which can help you ward off colds and keep your immune system healthy. Chocolate contains chemicals that can improve your mood. Too much sugar can make you feel run-down and cranky. The list below offers some suggestions for giving your body the foods you need to feel happier, more energetic, stronger, and healthier. Look at each picture and color the foods that you like in green, the foods that you would like to try in yellow, and the foods that you don't like as much in red.

FOOD TO IMPROVE YOUR MOOD

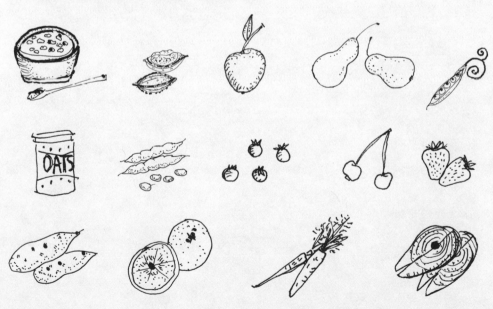

FOOD TO BOOST YOUR BRAIN AND MEMORY

FOOD TO SUSTAIN YOUR ENERGY

FOOD TO STRENGTHEN YOUR IMMUNE SYSTEM

Mom: Food Boosters

Look at each picture and color the foods that you like in green, the foods that you would like to try in yellow, and the foods that you don't like so much in red.

FOOD TO IMPROVE YOUR MOOD

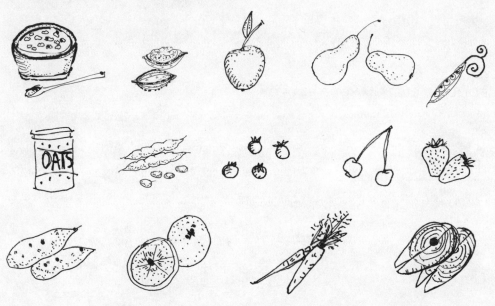

FOOD TO BOOST YOUR BRAIN AND MEMORY

FOOD TO SUSTAIN YOUR ENERGY

FOOD TO STRENGTHEN YOUR IMMUNE SYSTEM

Talk Time

What did you learn about food today?

What did you color in yellow and red?

After learning about different booster categories, is there any category you would like to try more foods from?

Is there anything in your diet that you would like to cut down on?

Let's Take a Breather

We will end this activity with a five-minute belly-breathing practice for mother and daughter to do together. Find a comfortable space to allow yourself to relax. You may open or close your eyes.

Take a slow, deep breath, filling up your belly—not your chest—with air. Now let it out slowly from your belly, gently pulling your belly back in so you push the air out. As you breathe in, say to yourself, *I am breathing in,* and as you breathe out, say to yourself, *I am breathing out.* When you are done you can smile at each other or give each other a high five!

let's ... Talk about Having a Positive Self-Image

Being a tween isn't easy or even a *little bit* simple. All of a sudden, other people's opinions seem extremely important, sometimes even more important than our own perceptions or beliefs about ourselves. Some girls are very self-conscious and afraid about acting, looking, or being different from their friends, especially the popular ones at school. If this has been your experience lately, congratulations on being a *tween*!

Even though this experience may feel difficult right now, remember that you are not alone! Most girls feel the same way you do even if they don't show it. And meanwhile, lots of moms feel powerless, frustrated, sad, and scared because their advice or opinion is no longer what their daughters want to hear.

Life gets complicated as you get older. There are so many pressures: other girls at school or in your neighborhood; images you see in magazines; clothes, fashion images, Victoria's Secret, Abercrombie & Fitch that you see at the mall; the Internet, your favorite TV shows or commercials; and the list goes on. You are still a kid, but it may feel like everything around you is pushing you to grow up.

Many tweens are easily confused about what society expects of them. For example, the idea of beauty gets magnified as if it is the only important thing that would make someone happy, popular, or successful. The messages we receive about beauty are expressed in a very limited and incomplete way, don't you think?

Because these messages seem so powerful, things like makeup, hair, body, nails, fashion, food, exercise, and relationships become the center of tween girls' conversations. These are normal topics, but don't forget that all of these things are external factors and interests, elements of your *outer* life that will eventually change or even become boring as you get older. Therefore, your number-one goal should be to focus on the *inner* qualities that make you beautiful, unique, special, and appreciated by others. For example, showing kindness sounds boring, but in fact it is one of the things people will appreciate about you the most throughout your life.

ABOUT THIS ACTIVITY

This exercise is designed to help you and your mom reflect on the qualities of being beautiful both on the inside and on the outside. It is important for you to know that the world is more interesting because everyone is different. In the first part of this activity, you will have a chance to think about your own physical characteristics and inner qualities that make you special, unique, and beautiful just the way you are. Then during the Talk Time section, you and your mom will make a cootie catcher together using a list of inner and outer qualities that you may want to consider working on together. (If you don't know what a cootie catcher is, stay tuned!)

EVEN MORE MINDFUL IDEAS

When you get caught in your own worries and fear, especially from outside pressure, and you find yourself worrying about what other people might be thinking about you, remind yourself to stay aware of your negative and unhealthy thoughts and feelings. Then ask yourself this question, *Am I being true to myself or do I just want to be like others?*

Daughter: Beautiful Inside and Outside

Take three minutes to come up with a list of physical characteristics that people often use to describe each other.

Take another three minutes to write down some of your external physical characteristics and some of your inner qualities that people have either complimented you on or criticized you for. Make sure you write something you like and don't like.

Take a few more minutes to really think about a couple of your inner qualities that you appreciate most about yourself and also think about the things that you would like to improve about yourself.

Mom: Beautiful Inside and Outside

Take three minutes to come up with a list of physical characteristics that people often use to describe each other.

Take another three minutes to write down some of your external physical characteristics and some of your inner qualities that people have either complimented you on or criticized you for. Make sure you write something you like and don't like.

Take a few more minutes to really think about a couple of your inner qualities that you appreciate most about yourself and also think about the things that you would like to improve about yourself.

Talk Time

The origami fortune-teller game is a fun way to help you recognize and focus on your positive qualities. In the game, you make an origami "cootie catcher," which has sides that are labeled with numbers and conceal messages under the flaps. In this game, the concealed messages will be the inner qualities or new habits that you want to possess or practice. Whatever inner quality or habit you each end up picking in the game, you need to practice for a day, a week, or whatever length of time you both agree on.

The next page will show you how to make the cootie catcher. Once you've made it, the two of you need to talk about which inner and outer qualities you want to put on the list that make you who you are: unique, special, and beautiful. You can list inner qualities or new habits that you want to work on—for example, "I want to take care of my hair every morning before I go to school" or "I will try to stop biting my nails" or "I will practice being more patient." Remember, it's what you think that matters the most! List these qualities in the space below.

1 _____

2 _____

3 _____

4 _____

5 _____

6 _____

7 _____

8 _____

After that, label each of the inside flaps of the origami with a number, and write one inner quality or new habit under each flap. Then decorate it! Take turns using the fortune-teller with your mom and enjoy being beautiful inside and out.

To make your cootie catcher, take a blank piece of paper and cut or fold it into a square. Then follow the steps in the diagram below.

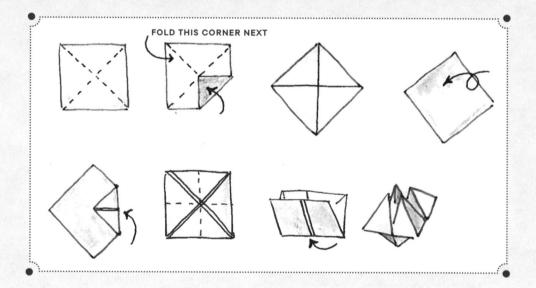

Let's Take a Breather

We will end this activity with a five-minute belly-breathing practice for mother and daughter to do together. Find a comfortable space to allow yourself to relax. You may open or close your eyes.

Take deep, slow, but comfortable breaths through your nose and let them out slowly through your mouth as if you are blowing big bubbles from your belly. As you breathe in say, "beautiful on the inside," and as you breathe out say, "beautiful on the outside." When you're done you can smile at each other or give each other a high five!

let's ... Spread Kindness

Kindness and happiness are strongly connected. When you act kindly, your body actually releases happy chemicals called "endorphins." Kind people tend to be happier, feel better about themselves, and have more true friends because they have learned the secret of putting themselves into somebody else's shoes.

You can express kindness in many ways. You can be helpful to others by letting them borrow your stuff or by giving away things you don't need. You can offer kind words or smiles. You can show respect by holding a door open or offering your seat to an elderly, disabled, or pregnant person. You can pick flowers from your backyard and give them to a friend. You can say "thank you" and "please" when you appreciate something that someone did for you. You can stick up for your friend when someone says something mean or not true about him or her. You can show that you care by asking a sad person if he or she needs any help. You can offer a tissue to someone who's crying. All of these small gestures can brighten up the world around you and make you feel wonderful inside and out.

Developing a kindness mind-set is an important life skill that is never too late to learn. Let's start now!

ABOUT THIS ACTIVITY

This activity is designed for you to experience the good feeling that come from doing something nice for others. You will create your own "kindness flyers" and hand them out to your family, friends, or adults you admire or respect. You can start by thinking of things that you would like to offer people that would put a smile on their face. It doesn't have to be something big or difficult, something that you'll have to go out of your way to do—it just needs to be something that would show a person that you appreciate him or her. For example, you could offer a hug or express how you feel about that person in a few words. Now, get creative and enjoy the happy moments that are about to happen. You will end your last activity together with a five-minute breathing practice for daughter and mom to do together. Be sure to stop and really take in the joy of being a giver.

EVEN MORE MINDFUL IDEAS

Watch your thoughts, feelings, and body sensations *before* and *after* you offer each random kindness. Good feelings and memories tend to last longer when you do a kind deed with all your heart and without expecting anything in return.

Daughter: Kindness Flyer

People often make flyers to post in public places to tell about an event, something for sale, or a lost pet. Take this time to create your own "kindness flyer," which can be posted at home or given to a friend or classmate at school or to someone you know. Think about what you want to offer people that would put a smile on their face. It's super nice to offer random kindness when people are least expecting it, and it is a great way to let them know how much you appreciate them. Scan and print or photocopy the kindness flyer, fill in the blank spaces, cut them up, pull off the tear-outs, and give them away to family members, friends, neighbors, or anyone you think is appropriate. Pay attention to people's reactions as well as to your own feelings.

FREE HUG (FAMILY)

THANK YOU FOR ALL YOU DO!!!! (ANYONE)

I LOVE YOU (FAMILY)

FREE MASSAGE (FAMILY)

HERE IS A PIECE OF CHOCOLATE (ANYONE)

Mom: Kindness Flyer

People often make flyers to post in public places to tell about an event, something for sale, or a lost pet. Take this time to create your own "kindness flyer," which can be posted at home or given to a friend or coworker or to someone you know. Think about what you want to offer people that would put a smile on their face. It is super nice to offer random kindness when people are least expecting it, and it is a great way to let them know how much you appreciate them. Scan and print or photocopy the kindness flyer, fill in the blank spaces, cut them up, pull off the tear-outs, and give them away to family members, friends, neighbors, or anyone you think is appropriate. Pay attention to people's reactions as well as to your own feelings.

FREE HUG (FAMILY)

THANK YOU FOR ALL YOU DO!!!! (ANYONE)

I LOVE YOU (FAMILY)

FREE MASSAGE (FAMILY)

HERE IS A PIECE OF CHOCOLATE (ANYONE)

Talk Time

Share with each other the creative kindness ideas you came up with.

Pick a tear-out from a kindness flyer and offer it to each other.
What is it like to be a giver? What is it like to be a receiver?

Let's Take a Breather

We will end this last activity with a five-minute belly-breathing practice for mother and daughter to do together. Find a comfortable space to allow yourself to relax. You may open or close your eyes.

Take a slow, deep breath, filling up your belly—not your chest—with air. Now let it out slowly from your belly, gently pulling your belly back in so you push the air out. Allow yourself to feel the joy of being a giver. As you breathe in, imagine yourself breathing in all the *appreciation* and *happiness* you have received from others. As you breathe out, send out *kindness* to all your family, your friends, and even people who might not be your favorites. When you are done you can smile at each other or give each other a hug.

Final Words

Hooray! You have now completed the whole workbook. You and your mom have done an amazing job learning and practicing the most essential life skills together. If you choose to continue practicing these skills, you will find yourself smiling more, feeling more confidence in yourself, feeling more connected to people at home and at school or at work, knowing how to handle big feelings or stressful events, and becoming much more mindful of your own thoughts, feelings, and the choices that you make.

More Tools

Talk Time Sign

You can make your own Talk Time Sign to use whenever you want to share important stuff or talk about a specific situation, or whenever mom or daughter needs some extra alone time with the other. The rule is that when mom or daughter presents this sign, the two of you need to find a quiet space to sit down together, listen carefully, and try to offer any help you can give.

Quiet Time Sign

Every once in a while, everyone—both kids and adults—needs to be alone and have quiet time. Alone time is precious time for you to be by yourself in a safe space, think through things, or rest and relax. Create a Quiet Time Sign that can be used to let others know that you need to take a break or recuperate.

Quiet Space Basket

The Quiet Space Basket will help you figure out what calms or soothes you when you have difficult moments. You will need to discover what items work for you. Look around your house to see if you have any of these items, or ask your mom to help you get some. Once you gather them, put them into a basket (a drawer or a bag would also be fine), and put the basket somewhere that you can easily access it. Pull out this basket anytime you need to take a break, are angry or tired, or want to relax or be alone. Each time you sit down, pick seven objects from the basket and find a quiet place to enjoy them.

Acknowledgments

Much of the inspiration for this book came from the special relationship I have with my own mom and what she has shown me throughout my life—perhaps most important, how crucial it is to pay attention to my mind and to live in the present moment. To her, I owe so very much.

I also would like to thank all of my clients, past and present, whose journey I feel deeply honored to be part of. You all are my best teachers. Many thanks to my supervisors and colleagues—Anne Gehrenbeck-Shim, PhD; Ayanna Quinones, PhD; Rhonda Kaplan; David Gleason, PsyD; and Jom Choomchuay, MD—for their knowledge, kindness, patience, and encouragement.

I also want to thank the editorial team at Shambhala, in particular Beth Frankl, Julia Gaviria, and Victoria Jones, for their sharp eyes and consistently superb suggestions. And a huge thank you goes to Lora Zorian for drawing the wonderful illustrations that have created the perfect setting for these activities.

References

Badeoch, B. (2008). *Being a Brain-Wise Therapist*. New York: W. W. Norton & Company.

Chödrön, P. (1991). *The Wisdom of No Escape and the Path of Loving-Kindness*. Boston: Shambhala Publications.

Criswell, P., and A. Martini (2013). *A Smart Girl's Guide: Friendship Troubles*. Middleton, WI: American Girl.

Cross, A. (2002). *Food Boosters for Kids*. London: Hamlyn.

Gruys, K. (2014). *Mirror, Mirror Off the Wall: How I Learned to Love My Body by Not Looking at It for a Year*. New York: Avery.

Harris, R. (2008). *The Happiness Trap: How to Stop Struggling and Start Living*. Boston: Trumpeter.

Harris, R., and S. Hayes (2009). *ACT Made Simple: An Easy-to-Read Primer on Acceptance and Commitment Therapy*. Oakland, CA: New Harbinger Publications.

Lawrence, S., and S. Robin (2009). *The Relaxation and Stress Reduction Workbook for Kids: Help for Children to Cope with Stress, Anxiety, and Transitions*. Oakland, CA: Instant Help Books.

Linehan, M. (1993). *Skill Training Manual for Treating Borderline Personality Disorder*. New York: Guilford Press.

"Raising a Girl with a Positive Body Image and Identity." PBS Parents online. Accessed May 26, 2015. www.pbs.org/parents /parenting/raising-girls/body-image-identity/raising-a-girl-with-a-positive-body-image/

Snel, E. (2014). *Sitting Still Like a Frog: Mindfulness Exercises for Kids*. Boston: Shambhala Publications.

About the Author

Nuanprang Snitbhan is a mother and clinical psychologist who specializes in working with children, adolescents, and their families. For over a decade, she has worked with kids from many different backgrounds in a variety of clinical and school settings. The most powerful tool that she offers parents and children is the skills for self-care and open communication in an environment that feels safe and gives them the confidence to grow together. She lives and practices in Boulder, Colorado.